BREATHE:

31 Moments with God
{for Moms}

JAIMIE BOWMAN

Purpose
Press

Published in Los Angeles, California by Purpose Press.

ISBN 978-0-9912325-0-5

Edited by Sandra Peoples – www.nextstepediting.com

Cover Photography by April Joy Gutel
Cover Design by Jaimie Bowman

FOR MY MOTHER

My many memories of you sitting with your Bible and your tea, early every morning, praying for our family, made an indelible impression on my soul. Thank you for putting Jesus first.

INTRODUCTION

After I became a mom, I struggled with how to feed my soul and spend time with God while I had two little ones running around. It seemed that every time I sat down for five minutes to read a passage, I would get interrupted and need to stop. Discouragement set in and I just gave up. I even dreaded going to church, because the amount of work it took to get there felt like I was preparing to run a marathon. Some big tantrum or blowout inevitably happened when I tried to leave the house. My soul longed to worship, to spend time with God and other believers, but sometimes I just felt like it was too much work. Pair that with the fact that I struggled with being disciplined as a whole, and my relationship with God suffered. I knew this was the time I needed Him the most, but I didn't know how to talk to Him or spend time with Him anymore.

Thankfully, a friend told me about the devotion book *Jesus Calling*, which was short enough yet deep enough to get me back into the habit of those daily devotions. It felt like water to my soul. God showed me new aspects of Himself and opened my eyes to the work He was doing around me, all while I was at home with my kids. There was so much He was doing in me, changing me and challenging me, but if I wasn't spending time with Him regularly, it would have been easy to miss.

My hope is that this little devotional will encourage you to get back into the practice of setting aside a time with God each day. Yes, you will probably be interrupted. It might be frustrating. But don't give up. I'm not a morning person, and no matter how hard I tried, waking before my kids just never worked for me. I wanted to start my day off right, though, so for me, their cartoon time was my devotional time. That won't work for everyone, so you'll have to be creative. Start with ten minutes and see how that goes. Maybe your time with God can be while nursing your baby, or while your kids are busy playing with a toy. Whatever time you can give, God will meet you there.

Let's not make it complicated, either. As a mom, you don't need further rules or restrictions on the time or place that you meet with God. Some days, take it outside while your kids are playing in the sand box. Other days you may find yourself awake ten minutes before the kids, and that is your time. Whenever and wherever you choose, God will meet you there.

This book has 31 days of devotionals that you may choose to read over again each month. They run about ten minutes each. Some devotions will have two or three verses, while some will include more. This is not meant to be your entire time with God for the day, but something to get you started. Use the thoughts and verses to springboard your prayers whispered throughout the day.

Also, there is a reason I have only included the Scripture references and not written the verses within the devotional.

I know for myself how easy it became to pick up a devotional and read it while my Bible sat on the shelf collecting dust. The Word of God is living and active, and there is power in picking up your Bible, feeling the pages between your fingers and reading it. Now, it is still powerful if it would have been written in this devotional. But I want you to get in the habit of turning those pages again, of marking your Bible with dates and verses that encourage you, and running to that as your source of encouragement throughout the day, not this little book.

My prayer is that God would use these verses to breathe into your soul and draw you closer to Him. My prayer is that He would use these words to encourage your heart, in whatever season of motherhood you are in. Thank you for the opportunity to speak into your life.

~Jaimie

Day 1

Read: Luke 8:22-25

Have you ever felt like you were drowning? Like you have been holding the weight of the world all on your own, and you can't handle even one more thing going wrong? As mothers, we often do this to ourselves. We commit and we serve and we volunteer and we help others, and we chauffeur and we clean and we cook and we try to do it all. Then we wonder why one day we feel like we're drowning.

Or maybe it's the situations completely out of our control that are causing us to drown—maybe it is our finances or our circumstances that feel so overwhelming.

In this Scripture passage, the disciples were in "great danger" (v. 23). They woke up Jesus and said, "We're going to drown!" It doesn't say they really asked Jesus for help; rather they informed Him of their impending doom. Jesus calmed the storm and then asked, "Where is your faith?" He wanted to know why, in the very midst of the storm, did they not see He was right there with them?

He is right there in the boat with us, too.

When you feel like you are sinking, is it because you are going to sink, or is it really because you haven't yet called on the Savior who is already in the boat?

When we call on Him, He calms the storm raging in our hearts. He may not choose to immediately fix the circumstance we're in, and He may not answer the way we would like Him to, yet He can still calm that storm inside. It is possible to have a calm heart while the storm is raging outside.

So today, when the bills pile up around you, He is with you.

When the children are sick and need you every minute, He is with you.

When you don't know how you are going to get it all done, He is with you.

When you're worried about decisions your child is making, He is with you.

When you are burdened and overwhelmed by the trials of life, He is with you.

He is right there with you in the boat. Just call on His name.

PRAYER:

God, I need You in this moment. Help me to remember to call on Your name, the One who can calm the storm, the One who can bring peace to my soul. You are there with me, even when I cannot see You or feel You. Bring Your peace into my family today, into my home. Strengthen my faith so I will no longer feel like I'm drowning, but know You are beside me.

REFLECTION QUESTIONS:

- Is there anything happening in your life that makes you feel like you are drowning?

- Have you called on the Lord for help, and are you trusting Him with this area in your life?

- How might God use this situation to strengthen your faith in Him?

_____

_____

_____

_____

_____

_____

_____

_____

_____

_____

_____

_____

_____

_____

Day 2

Read: Galatians 5:19-25

It is interesting to me that some of the most common issues we struggle with as mothers are wedged right in the middle of these verses, in between sexual immorality, idolatry, and witchcraft. I just have a hard time seeing my jealousy of another mother's awesome diaper bag as serious as someone committing adultery, yet it's right there in the midst of the other evil acts. Verse 20 also says that discord is an act of the sinful nature. Discord? As in, disagreeing with my husband? Jealousy? And fits of rage? Well, my three-year-old and I know *all about* fits of rage. Then there's envy ... don't even get me started on my envy of the mom at preschool who said she potty-trained her child as an infant.

"But the fruit of the Spirit is love, joy, peace, patience, kindness, goodness, faithfulness, gentleness and self-control" (v. 22-23). The fruit of the Spirit is given to us by the Holy Spirit to combat those evil desires that war within us. Our sinful nature will always be there, telling us we don't need to change ... we don't need to be loving ... we don't need to crucify our old selves.

Being a mother is like being in the refiner's fire. Daily we are faced with situations in which we can choose to respond according to our old-nature (before Christ) or our new-nature (after Christ).

I remember meeting with an older woman who said to me, "Be thankful when your child throws a tantrum! Thank God that He is refining you and making you more like Him through your little boy." Really? Is that even possible? But it's true. There is nothing that will press you, mold you, shape you, and conform you into the likeness of Christ more than a temperamental toddler or teenager—that is, *if* we allow Christ to do His work in us. We can become so set on changing our children's behavior that we overlook the fact that Christ is trying to change our own behavior as well.

Next time you are in a battle with your child, ask God to teach you, train you, and mold you into His likeness. Thank Him for refining your character, for attempting to give you the fruit of the Spirit. It's not easy to respond that way, but God wants to teach us about Himself and about ourselves through the relationships we have with our children.

PRAYER:

God, You know my struggles. You know when I am envious, jealous, and angry. Please make me more like You today. Help me to see my child as an instrument of You in my life to make me more like You. I long to develop Your fruit in my life. Help me to respond to my family with love, joy, peace, patience, kindness, goodness, faithfulness, gentleness, and self-control. I submit myself to You and ask You to change me from the inside out. Thank You.

REFLECTION QUESTIONS:

- Which one of the fifteen sins listed in Galatians 5:19-25
  do you feel you need to work on the most?

- Which fruit of the Spirit do you feel you need to work on
  the most?

- How might those be related?

_____

_____

_____

_____

_____

_____

_____

_____

_____

_____

_____

_____

_____

_____

_____

_____

Day 3

Lamentations 3:22-26

It was the Friday before Mother's Day when I picked my preschooler up from school. He handed me a small, wrapped present with his four-year-old hands and asked, "Mommy, where were you?" I looked in the classroom and could see the other moms, dressed up and looking like they had been there awhile. Then it dawned on me ... I had just missed the Mother's Day tea. I was the *only mother* who had missed the Mother's Day tea. Tears filled my eyes as I realized what I had done. How could I have forgotten? I approached the teacher to offer my heartfelt apology and she told me my son sat on her lap the entire time and was fine, but in my mind I was thinking, "My son had to sit on your lap because I was the only mom not there?!" I was horrified. I took my son to the park afterward and tried to console him. Honestly, he was fine, but I was not. It took months for me to even be able to think about that day without crying.

Mommy guilt. It's serious business. Mommy guilt is that feeling of remorse you get after you've made a mistake, dealt too harshly with your children, or were unable to protect them when they needed you. It comes in many forms and at the most inconvenient times. If we are not careful, mommy guilt can hang over us like a heavy blanket, leading to feelings of regret, anxiety, and even depression.

It can also be sneaky; mommy-guilt is not a respecter of events or even truth. Even when we have no control over an outcome, and there is nothing more we could have done, it can still hang in the background of our hearts.

Lamentations 3:22-24 reminds us gently that our forgetfulness, our failures, our mistakes—they do not need to consume us. Verse 22 says the Lord loves us and has compassion on us. His compassions, His mercies, are *new every morning*. What an encouragement to those of us who struggle with failures we have had in the past, even when they were just yesterday.

Verse 25 goes on to say "the Lord is good to those whose hope is in Him; to the one who seeks Him." We need to put our hope back in the Lord, because every time we put our hope in ourselves—that we will be everything our children need—we will come up short. Our hope, and our children's hope, should first be in the Lord. Take heart today, dear mother—His mercies are new every morning.

PRAYER:

Lord, every day I come up short. I fail in many ways. Yet You are faithful to me, even in my weaknesses. Thank You for Your love, Your compassion, and Your mercy. I release my guilt to You, and ask that You replace that feeling with Your unending grace. As You wash over my heart with grace, help me to extend that to my family members as well. Thank You for Your mercies that are new every morning.

REFLECTION QUESTIONS:

- What is something you carry around mommy guilt for?

- How has that guilt consumed you at times?

- Can you come to a place where you receive God's grace for your mistakes, and can you let them go?

_____

_____

_____

_____

_____

_____

_____

_____

_____

_____

_____

_____

_____

_____

_____

_____

DAY 4

Read: John 13:1-17

There may come a time when your child will hurt your feelings, refuse the dinner you worked so hard on, or act like he doesn't care about your existence anymore ... you, the very one who gave them life. And yet at the end of the day, you will find yourself giving that child a bath, washing his little toes, pouring the clean water over his body. If she is older, you might find yourself washing her clothes, putting her shoes away, or packing her lunch. Sometimes they take and don't give in return, and sometimes it hurts.

When Jesus washed His disciples' feet, He did so not expecting anything in return. Jesus chose to wash the feet of two men who would betray Him: Judas and Simon Peter. Those feet were dirty and they smelled; but worse than anything, those were the feet of those who would deny His very existence and deny everything He had done for them.

In washing the disciples' feet, Jesus taught us to forgive, to love, and to have grace on those who may not deserve it. Jesus was their master, yet He took the role of the slave in choosing to wash their feet.

It is tempting, in all that we do for our children, to feel sorry for ourselves. We don't get the appreciation we should. We rarely get anything in return. We may find ourselves mistreated. In Jesus' example, however, He did not retaliate. He did not seek to make their lives miserable. He chose to take the higher road and serve them in love.

When you feel discouraged about the many ways you serve your family that might get overlooked, remember the example Jesus set for us. He served in love, not getting frustrated when others didn't notice His efforts. He didn't retaliate, He forgave. When we serve our families, we are following Jesus' example: we are washing their feet. We are stooping down to do the dirty work, the work nobody else will do, the work of a servant—not because we have to, but because Jesus called us to this task. He showed us how to serve in love. In verse 14, He says, "Now that I, your Lord and Teacher, have washed your feet, you also should wash one another's feet."

What an honor that we are given the opportunity to wash the feet of our family members today, just as Jesus modeled for us.

PRAYER:

Lord, I want to serve out of love—not out of obligation, duty, or frustration. I pray You would help me to have the right attitude and heart about my service today. Remind me that as I meet my family's needs, that I am washing their feet, just as You did for the disciples that day. Thank you for this honor You have given me.

REFLECTION QUESTIONS:

- When was a time your child hurt your feelings or you worked hard, and he or she didn't acknowledge your hard work?

- Do you ever find yourself serving your family while expecting something in return?

- How can you serve your family today in love?

_____

_____

_____

_____

_____

_____

_____

_____

_____

_____

_____

_____

_____

_____

_____

DAY 5

Read: Isaiah 40: 28-31

Christie's daughter had a long day and fell asleep on the couch two hours before her bedtime. Christie couldn't tell who was more exhausted though, herself or her daughter. She quietly wished she could just fall asleep like that, but knew she had a few more hours to go before she could turn out the lights.

Early motherhood is marked with exhaustion. It can be difficult to get through the day when you've only had a few hours of sleep, most of which were interrupted by a baby needing to nurse or a child having a bad dream. We subsist on caffeine, chocolate, or anything we can find that might give us that extra strength we need until we can find time to rest.

The good news is that God's strength never runs out—He never gets tired or weary. But how do we access *His* strength in order to get the strength *we* need? Oftentimes instead of making that connection, we continue going on through our day just trying to get by, not realizing we have His ever-present power there to help us.

When we are at our lowest point, we can call on Him for the energy and power we need to get through the day. Feeling weary? He promises to give us strength. Feeling weak?

He promises to increase our power.

Verse 31 says when we hope in the Lord, our strength is renewed. Isaiah gives the analogy of an eagle soaring. Did you know when a storm is coming, an eagle uses that wind to fly higher? He doesn't fly away from the wind, but instead flies right *into it*. That wind is what propels him to soar.

Isaiah says the key to having our strength renewed is to hope in the Lord (v. 31). When our hope is in Him, and not in ourselves, we will find a renewed strength. Our day-to-day responsibilities don't need to overwhelm us if we are relying on Christ's power to help us.

We also don't have to be afraid of the storms that come our way. We can face them head-on, because we know God will enable us with the strength and power we need.

It is okay to be tired. It is okay to admit you are worn out. Yet instead of feeling defeated, remember you can simply call on the One who has everlasting strength and power, and He will give you the strength to endure.

PRAYER:

God, I need Your strength. I cannot do this on my own. Some days my head is swimming with everything I need to do, and yet I am only one person. Today I put my hope and my trust in You. You have all the strength I need for today. I ask You to renew my strength as I trust in You and not in myself. Thank You that *You* never grow tired or weary.

REFLECTION QUESTIONS:

- What causes you to feel weary and tired?

- What have you been relying on to give you strength?

- Read verse 31 again. How do you think you can place your hope in the Lord today?

_____

_____

_____

_____

_____

_____

_____

_____

_____

_____

_____

_____

_____

_____

_____

_____

DAY 6

Read: Matthew 6:25-34

Have you ever stayed awake at night worrying about your children? Perhaps you worried about their health, their decisions, their friendships, their education ... the list can go on for days. When my boys were newborns, my husband and I worried about every little thing. We would rush them to the doctor only to find out that the baby was perfectly normal, developing right on track. As they grow older, we find there are new things to worry about. Now it's not so much if they are breathing correctly at night, but about their schooling and their friendships.

Worrying seems to come natural for moms. Yet it is also something Christ commands us not to do. How do we stop something we seem to have no control over?

Apparently it is possible to not worry, otherwise Jesus wouldn't have instructed us not to do so. Worrying has many effects on our health, and many studies have pointed to a correlation between worrying and shorter life spans. So Jesus was telling us in verse 27 that by not worrying, we are actually improving our life expectancy. That alone should make us want to work on this area in our lives, so we will be around longer for our children.

Verse 32 and 33 give the answer we need in order to combat worry. Jesus tells us that our Heavenly Father knows what we need, and we need to seek Him first.

You see, when we put Christ first in our lives and our attention is on Him, we don't need to worry so much. It is when our eyes are off of Christ and on our circumstance, on our earthly affairs, that worry and anxiety set in. So in regard to our children, we have to daily choose to give them over to the Lord. Worrying is not going to add one more hour to our lives; in fact, it will adversely affect our lives. It is imperative that we learn how to control these worries and trust Christ.

Worry can hinder us from moving forward, while concern can propel us to move forward. So it's okay to be concerned, but we have to be careful not to let it turn into worry.

Of course this is easier said than done. But next time you are struggling, and worry is keeping you awake at night, choose at that moment to remember these words. If God cares for the birds of the air, how much more does He care for us and for our children? He will provide all that we need, emotionally, physically, and spiritually.

PRAYER:

Jesus, I come to You with all of my worries and cares right now. Help me to lay them at Your feet. I don't want to be consumed with these things; I want to trust You more. You will provide for all I need. You are faithful. I praise You that You are in control and as I seek You, You will answer.

REFLECTION QUESTIONS:

- What is something you worry about on a regular basis?

- How are your worries affecting you emotionally, physically or spiritually?

- Do you feel that you are trusting Christ with your concerns, or holding on to them?

_____

_____

_____

_____

_____

_____

_____

_____

_____

_____

_____

_____

_____

_____

_____

DAY 7

Read: Exodus 2:1-10

Imagine for a few minutes the fear that Moses' mother must have gone through in this story. First, she fears for her son's life because all of the baby boys are going to be murdered. In the close-knit community she lived in, there was no doubt who all the new babies were. Mothers in that day spent their days together, helping each other and raising each other's babies. There really was no good hiding place if a mother wanted to protect her infant from this decree. Moses' mother was smart, though; she used her skill to weave a basket, and her ingenuity to think of a place she could hide him—she would place him in the basket and put him in the river. Think of the agony she must have felt, placing her beautiful baby boy inside of that basket and *letting him go*. The Scripture says that when Moses was found, he was crying. Can you imagine her mother's heart, hearing her baby cry and not being able to comfort him?

She was afraid, but she left her baby in God's hands.

Sometimes that is all we can do. We try our best to be the mothers our kids need us to be, but sometimes it just isn't enough. We have to let them go, and that is where God steps in.

We will face many situations throughout our children's lives that will test our faith and require us to ask ourselves, "Do I really trust God with my child?" We will be tempted to hold on to them, even in situations in which God might ask us to let go. In our fear, we may try to keep our children in situations where we can control them, rather than trusting that God is in control of their lives.

When Moses' mother let him go, she released him into God's hands, and into the plan that God had created for Moses' life. It took courage and faith for her to make that hard decision, but God blessed Moses' life because of it.

Before our children were given to us, they were God's children first. He loves your child with a love that is even greater than the human love we have for our own. Our fears are no match for His great strength. Just as God watched over Moses and protected his life, He will watch over our own. You can trust Him.

PRAYER:

God, sometimes I have a hard time letting my child go. I want to protect her, I want to shield her from all harm. If there is a situation in which I am holding my child back from what You want, please show me. Remind me my child is Your child first, and You will guard and protect her because You have a plan for her life. Help me to trust You.

REFLECTION QUESTIONS:

- What speaks to your heart the most about Moses' story in this passage?

- In what ways might God ask you to let your child go in the coming years?

- Do you trust God with your child?

_____

_____

_____

_____

_____

_____

_____

_____

_____

_____

_____

_____

_____

_____

_____

_____

Day 8

Read: Philippians 4:4-7

When was the last time you felt peace? I don't mean quietness; I mean *peace*, inside of your soul; the kind of peace that only comes from God. Sometimes we equate silence with peace, but you can sit in a quiet room and still have turmoil inside of your heart. What is bothering you today? What circumstance or person is dividing your attention and trying to steal the peace God longs to give you?

Paul gives four instructions in this passage that reap a valuable result: the peace of God.

First, Paul says to rejoice—not in our circumstances, or that we accomplished our to-do list for the day—but rather to rejoice *in the Lord, always*. Many times we don't feel like we can rejoice because our eyes are on our situations instead of on God.

Second, verse five says we are to be gentle, and that our gentleness should be evident to all. Oh sure, we are quick to be gentle and patient with our children when we are in public, but are we that way at home too, away from the eyes of others? Paul reminds us that the Lord is near—He sees all.

Third, verse six admonishes us to not be anxious about

anything. How do we stop anxiety over things we have no control over? We submit those things to God; we trust that He is in control.

Lastly, he tells us to present our requests to God, but with an attitude of thanksgiving. A mark of spiritual maturity is the ability to thank God in advance for His answer, even when it may not be what we asked for.

If we do these things, verse seven says we *will* experience the peace of God—a peace that is beyond understanding—and it will guard our hearts and minds in Christ Jesus. The Greek word for "guard" means to protect. Our hearts will be protected from anxiety and worry when we experience the peace of God that comes from obeying Him.

Which one of these four instructions that Paul gives is the hardest for you to obey? If you were to ask me, I would have to say all of them! When we are not experiencing peace in our hearts, the first place to look is within ourselves. Are we rejoicing in the Lord? Do we have gentle attitudes? Are we anxious about something? Are we thankful? Usually one of these can be the root of a lack of peace in our lives.

PRAYER:

Jesus, I need Your peace. Help me, oh God, to rejoice in You, not in my circumstances. Let gentleness fill my heart and mind so that it overflows to my family. Help me not to be anxious but to trust fully in You and Your plan. I also ask You to give me a heart of thanksgiving. As I obey You, will

You fill my heart with the peace that only You can give?
I submit my worries to You and thank You for Your peace.

REFLECTION QUESTIONS:

- When was the last time you felt peace?

- What is holding you back from rejoicing in the Lord
  always?

- Which one of the four instructions that Paul gives is
  hardest for you to obey?

_____

_____

_____

_____

_____

_____

_____

_____

_____

_____

_____

_____

_____

_____

_____

_____

_____

_____

_____

_____

_____

_____

_____

_____

_____

_____

_____

_____

_____

_____

_____

_____

_____

_____

_____

DAY 9

Read: Psalm 139:1-10

I was tucking my six–year-old son into bed when he quietly asked me a question, "Mom, what if He lets go of my hand?" It took me a moment to figure out what he was asking. "If who lets go of your hand?" I asked. "God," he softly replied.

Earlier in the week we had a conversation about some issues he was having at school, and I had commented that Jesus was always holding his hand, and he did not need to be afraid. That conversation had weighed on his heart, and so he had a valid question: "What if He lets go of my hand?"

As I consoled him and reassured him that God would never let go of his hand, I was reminded that there have been times that I have asked the same question: "What if God lets go of me?"

No matter how old we get, and how mature we are in our faith, things happen in our lives that may make us wonder if God has forgotten about us—if He has, indeed, let go of our hands. We may feel alone, not hear His voice, and be confused. Yet Psalm 139 reminds us of God's constant presence in our lives. Even if we *try* to escape from His presence, He is still there.

Just because we don't feel His presence physically does not mean He has left our sides. Verse 5 says God "hems" us in, behind and before: He encloses us in, He enwraps us in His presence. Whether we are having a great day or a terrible day (v. 8), His hand is there to guide us.

There are moments in our parenting when we may genuinely feel like God has let go of our hands. We may not know what to do in a certain situation, and we fail to hear His clear voice, and so we feel like He has left us. We may not see God at work, and we may not understand why bad things happen. Yet not understanding the purposes of God does not mean that His presence has left us alone.

Be encouraged today that God knows you intimately, He is with you, and He has not left you alone.

PRAYER:

Oh God, I realize that I do not fully understand Your ways. I cannot even comprehend the love You have for me. I confess there are times my faith falters, because I don't feel You or hear Your voice clearly. Give me a steadfast heart that will trust and know that You will never leave me or forsake me. Thank You for Your constant presence in my life. Open my eyes to see and hear You today.

REFLECTION QUESTIONS:

- Have you ever felt like God left you alone?

- Looking back, are you able to see His presence still with you during that time?

- How has this Scripture encouraged you today?

_____

_____

_____

_____

_____

_____

_____

_____

_____

_____

_____

_____

_____

_____

_____

DAY 10

Read: Genesis 3:1-7

Here we come to the story of Adam and Eve, and Eve's fateful decision to eat the fruit from the Tree of Knowledge of Good and Evil. If Eve only knew the ramifications that choice would have on her and future generations, she likely would not have chosen to take a bite. But isn't that the truth for most of us? We don't think about the ramifications of our sin, and so we go ahead and do it. We are not thinking ahead to the possible consequences upon ourselves and our families.

But Eve's greatest struggle is often overlooked, and that is the root of what led her to make this choice in the first place. When we are discontent, we are always looking at what we do not have and wishing it was ours. Rather than focusing on the abundant blessings God has given to us, we remain fixated on the one or two big things we feel will bring us happiness and contentment.

Eve was in the most beautiful of environments, surrounded by lush gardens, all of the food she could want, and a husband who loved her. Yet she was not content and desired the one thing God told her she should not have. She rationalized her desire, listened to the voice of the serpent who told her she needed it, and gave in.

The serpent appealed to three needs Eve had (in verse 6): her appetite (the fruit was good for food), her sight (it was beautiful), and her desire for knowledge and power (she would gain wisdom). Once she ate, her husband also took a bite, and then they hid from the Lord. Her decision impacted multiple people, including her future children who would never experience life in the garden.

What temptations do you fight against on a regular basis? It is things that are pleasing to the eye (materialism), or the appetite (perhaps food or drink that is not good for us, or even an appetite for unholy desires), or is it a desire for power? If we are not careful, we can rationalize our decisions and go after things that will hurt us. Those decisions also make us want to run and hide from God.

Pray that your eyes will be opened to any sins that might be distracting you from your purpose as a child of God, and ask that God would help you to submit those areas to Him.

PRAYER:

Father, help me to be completely content with all that You have given me. Open my eyes to see the many blessings You have surrounded me with. I get distracted easily and want what I do not have. Give me strength against temptation and sin—against wanting things that ultimately will not bring me happiness or peace. Help me to find my contentment solely in You.

REFLECTION QUESTIONS:

- What are some things you lack that you feel would bring you happiness?

- What sins might be distracting you from God's purposes for you?

- How have you rationalized some of those sins?

_____

_____

_____

_____

_____

_____

_____

_____

_____

_____

_____

_____

_____

_____

_____

DAY 11

Read: John 9:1-11

Has something ever happened to your child that made you feel like it was your fault?

When my oldest son was two years old, we realized that he had a significant speech delay. It concerned us, so we took him to be tested. My husband and I felt like we were on an emotional roller-coaster. Those months of not knowing what was going on, wondering if our child would be affected for life, made me feel like a horrible mother. I hated seeing my child go through the testing process, having to cart him around to different specialists. I wondered if I hadn't done enough, if he had watched too much television, if we had played our music too loud—you name it.

After months of uncertainty, we visited a specialist who said he had residual fluid in his ears from multiple ear infections. We had our answer, our son had surgery, and his hearing and speech are now where they should be.

At the time, that felt like the longest and hardest trial we had ever been through. We pleaded with God, we blamed ourselves and begged Him to heal our son.

The parents in this passage had a son who was blind from birth. If you read closely though, you see it was not the parents who asked Jesus the difficult question, but rather the disciples. *They* wanted to know what the parents had done to cause this child to go blind. Sometimes dealing with the judgment of others is worse than the judgment we heap upon ourselves.

Jesus' answer was gentle and full of love: "Neither this man nor his parents sinned,' said Jesus, 'but this happened so that the work of God might be displayed in his life."

What situation are you or your child facing today that seems impossible? If I could sit with you and encourage you, it would be with these words: God will give you grace for this season, and the work of God will be displayed in your lives. That situation we went through with our son was hard, but God revealed His character to us during that time. We became closer to Him as He was our only option for peace and security. He opened many doors to minister to others as I came to empathize with others in similar situations.

We may not always understand why God allows us or our children to experience hardship, but we can remain confident that His work will be completed, and He will give us the strength to endure.

PRAYER:

Lord, help me not to be focused on what others might think, or be overcome with fear over my child's health or future. I give my child to You and ask that Your will be accomplished in his life. Help me to trust that You have a purpose and a plan for my child in every difficult season. May Your work be accomplished in our lives.

REFLECTION QUESTIONS:

- When was a time that you felt responsible for something your child experienced, that may or may not have been your fault?

- If there has been a particular hardship that your family has faced, how have you seen God work in that situation?

- What current situation are you having a hard time accepting?

_____

_____

_____

_____

_____

_____

_____

_____

_____

_____

_____

DAY 12

Read: 2 Corinthians 12:7-10

It started out so innocently. I logged onto Facebook just for a minute, but it was the first post I saw: "Wow! Cleaned the entire house today, got the oil changed in the car, made my own organic baby food, played with the kids, made an amazing dinner, gave them all baths, and had them in bed by 7:30pm. I feel like Superwoman!"

Well, good for her. This was one of the days I wasn't feeling like Superwoman, and that didn't help a bit. My mind took off, and before I knew it, I was caught up again in the daily "comparison trap." This trap often derails my entire day, as I start to feel down about myself and hopeless about all the things I could be doing better. Pretty soon I find myself sitting on top of a pile of laundry instead of folding it, because "why bother?" I will never be Superwoman like her.

Yet God speaks to my heart in that moment, "My grace is sufficient for you, for my power is made perfect in weakness." (v. 9) When I start thinking about my weaknesses, all of them, He reminds me to look up. When I take my eyes off of myself, and focus on His grace, I am able to begin to work on these things. I have to have my eyes on Him only.

Sometimes God uses everyday conversations and events to

deal with issues in our own hearts. I needed God to work on this weed in my life and get it out by the roots. Comparison is deadly, it is toxic, and it changes us. It turns us into people who are fake, who want to be better than others, who are bitter, and who resent the strengths of other people. Comparison is a tool Satan uses to take the focus off of God onto ourselves.

Next time you are tempted to focus on the feats of others, their superhuman abilities or their stellar mothering skills, remember that He has grace for you. As Paul had a thorn in his flesh, we all have issues in our lives that are like thorns. Yet God reminds us that His grace is sufficient. He wants to display His power through our weaknesses.

Focus today on His grace, for it is enough. He is able to show Himself through our weaknesses. It's okay to be real, it's okay to admit our weaknesses, because those are the areas where He can still get glory. Instead of trying to be Superwoman today, allow God to be your strength and don't worry about trying to impress anybody else.

PRAYER:

Father, I struggle with comparison sometimes. I look at other women and all that they can accomplish, and I wish I could do those things too. I know my weaknesses, yet I don't want others to see them. Help me to be broken, to be honest and open, and to give those weaknesses to You so You can change me. Remind me today that I am *enough* in Your eyes.

REFLECTION QUESTIONS:

- Do you ever struggle with comparison? If so, in what ways?

- How do you feel comparison changes people?

- What areas of weakness in yourself do you have a hard time with?

_____

_____

_____

_____

_____

_____

_____

_____

_____

_____

_____

_____

_____

_____

_____

_____

_____

_____

_____

_____

_____

_____

_____

_____

_____

_____

_____

_____

_____

_____

_____

_____

_____

_____

_____

_____

_____

_____

_____

_____

DAY 13

Read: I Peter 4:8-11

"Above all, love each other deeply" (v. 8).

I don't know about you, but there are plenty of days when I don't do a good job of loving my family well. Oh, I may love them in my heart, but my words and my actions don't really show it. We would do well if, when our children were grown, they would be able to look back and know their parents loved them deeply.

What I love about this section of Scripture is that it speaks to so many of the issues we face in motherhood.

In verse 8, we are reminded to "love each other deeply, because love covers over a multitude of sins." That begs a question, however—should a multitude of sins really be covered up? Should my children just get away with what they are doing wrong? That is not what this verse is implying; rather, it is saying when we love deeply, we are able to forgive easier, to move forward, to not hold our children's sins against them—just as Christ loves us.

In verse 9, we are instructed to "offer hospitality to one another without grumbling." We often interpret this verse to apply to church potlucks and such, yet it is applicable to us as well, in our ministry as mothers. We offer hospitality to our families every day as we serve them; but are we doing it without complaining and without grumbling?

Verse 10 reminds us to use our gifts to serve others, because it is a way to "administer God's grace in its various forms." What a privilege we have to serve our families in this way, using the gifts God has given us to show our families the way God loves and serves us. You may not know you have gifts—that God has given you strengths as a mother—but He has.

In verse 11, Peter reminds us that when we speak, we "should do it as one speaking the very words of God." We have that much power in our children's lives—to speak into their tender hearts with love and grace. Are our words full of love and grace, or full of anger and frustration?

In all that we do, may we seek to glorify God and honor Him through our words and actions.

PRAYER:

God, I ask You today to help me to love my family deeply, in a way that they would know Your love for them and my love for them as well. Remind me, as I grow weary, that I need to serve them with the strength You provide, not with my own. May You help me to walk in Your love today as I seek to honor You in all that I do.

REFLECTION QUESTIONS:

- How are you doing on loving your family well today?

- Are there any sins or mistakes your family members have made that you are having a hard time forgiving?

- What are some gifts or strengths you have as a mother?

_____

_____

_____

_____

_____

_____

_____

_____

_____

_____

_____

_____

_____

_____

_____

_____

DAY 14

Read: I Samuel 1:21-28

I suppose dropping your child off to kindergarten for the first time feels a bit like dropping your child off at college for the first time. Although I haven't yet experienced the college drop-off, many friends of mine have and can attest to the nervous stomach, the inability to sleep for awhile, the crying (and crying, and crying), and general fear of the unknown. After spending years of caring for our children's every need, it can be one of the hardest parts of parenting to watch them walk off into the unknown. Yet seeing them grow into the young men and women God has called them to be is also an exciting and amazing experience.

I wonder if Hannah experienced any of those emotions as she left her son Samuel to live with the high priest. Hannah had been unable to have children, and so Samuel was a surprise and special blessing from the Lord.

If you are unfamiliar with this story, I encourage you to read all of I Samuel chapters 1-2. Because Hannah was so blessed by the gift God had given to her, she made a decision to give her son back to the Lord: she would send him to live in the temple and be raised by the high priest so he would serve the Lord his entire life. In biblical times, a child was considered weaned around two or three years of age, so when Hannah brought her son to the temple to live, he was very small. In verses 28-29, she says, "I prayed for this child, and the Lord has granted me what I asked of Him. So now I give him to the Lord. For his whole life he will be given over to the Lord."

Now, most of us cannot imagine making a decision like that—it almost seems like abandonment! Yet Hannah's heart was to give her child back to God as an offering for all He had done for her. It was a true act of love and sacrifice for her to make that decision.

We may find ourselves so far removed from this story that it is hard to relate. But I believe this passage would beg to ask us: Have we given our children back to the Lord? Many of us would probably say we have; we may have even had a baby dedication ceremony. But have we truly given our children over to the Lord and trusted Him with their lives?

I know for myself, I am tempted to hold on to my children tightly. I don't want anything bad to happen to them; I want to protect them. But Hannah's example teaches us to daily present our children to God as an offering—that they would be used by Him for His purposes.

PRAYER:

God, help me to trust You enough to give my children to You – their hearts, their bodies, their souls and their minds. I don't want to control their lives, but to release them into Your care, that You would use them as You desire. Help me to have the faith, bravery and courage of Hannah, that I would surrender my children to you.

REFLECTION QUESTIONS:

- What is something you waited a long time for an answer about?

- Have you ever made a conscious decision in your heart to give your child to the Lord, as Hannah did?

- What area of your child's life do you struggle with trusting God about?

_____

_____

_____

_____

_____

_____

_____

_____

_____

_____

_____

_____

_____

_____

Day 15

Read: Luke 18:15-17

Renee was reading a devotional to her five year old son when they started to discuss the crucifixion and how the soldiers killed Jesus. D. J. told his mother the soldiers "didn't unlock their hearts to Jesus—but I did, you did, and daddy did, so we get to be with Jesus in heaven someday." Renee nodded in agreement as D. J. continued explaining his perspective, that everyone has a little key to unlock their hearts to Jesus. He said, "a little Jesus comes down, jumps in your mouth—if you let Him—goes down your throat to your heart, gets the key, opens the door, walks in, and then lives and grows in your heart."

Don't you love the innocence of children and their childlike faith? That may not be exactly how it happens, but he gets the point. Children can teach us a lot about faith.

Many of us started out in our Christian walks with a childlike faith, a wonder at His works, and a simple, uncomplicated belief that He was present and would hear our prayers.

Somewhere along the way, often through trials in our lives, discouragement sets in and begins to chip away at that childlike faith. We doubt God's faithfulness and His love for us. We question His character and His goodness.

Jesus tells us in Matthew 18 that we should become like little children. So how do we go back to having that childlike faith again? It starts with believing—uncomplicated belief, just like D. J. had. He wasn't making faith complicated, and his faith was no-strings-attached; he was simply believing.

Having a childlike faith is not immaturity. A childlike faith is simple and teachable. It is not needing to know all of the answers. It is trusting instead of trying to control.

Jesus didn't mince any words in this passage; He said if we do not receive the kingdom of God like a little child, we will never enter it. A childlike faith is not just a one-time act that happens when we accept Jesus into our hearts. Throughout our Christian walks, we need to work at *keeping* a childlike faith.

The next time you notice your child's simple faith, ask God to create that kind of faith in you again. Surrender your questions, fears and doubts to Him, and go back to the faith you once knew.

PRAYER:

Jesus, teach me more about You and Your character through my own children. I long for that kind of childlike faith that trusts in You and loves You without condition. Renew in me a simple heart, and give me eyes to see You with the faith of a child. Thank You.

REFLECTION QUESTIONS:

- How have you seen childlike faith displayed in your own son or daughter?

- Think back to when your faith began. At what point did that childlike faith start to be replaced with fear or worry?

- What is keeping you from having a childlike faith once again?

_____

_____

_____

_____

_____

_____

_____

_____

_____

_____

_____

_____

_____

_____

DAY 16

Read: Colossians 3: 18-25

The title of this passage of Scripture is "Rules for Christian Households." Don't you wish we had an instruction manual for raising children? A list of rules that would help us know what to do in every situation? The Bible is full of wisdom, advice, and even rules for Christian households to follow, but it's not always easy to know how to apply those verses to certain situations we find ourselves in.

Paul starts out by giving instructions to wives, then husbands, then children, then fathers, and lastly slaves (as slaves were a common household occurrence in that day). Yet where is the specific advice for mothers? Where is our little nugget of wisdom?

I believe verses 23-24 speak directly to the heart of mothers: "Whatever you do, work at it with all your heart, as working for the Lord, not for men, since you know that you will receive an inheritance from the Lord as a reward. It is the Lord Christ you are serving."

You see, when we are called to motherhood, we are called to a holy task. God gifts us with these children to shape their hearts and souls for eternity, and to lead them toward Himself. When we speak, we teach them about the heart of God. When we serve, we serve as unto Christ. When we make their lunches and tie their shoes and wipe their faces, we can do it as though we are serving Christ Himself.

Sometimes we can also get resentful over the fact that in all we do for our kids, we are not making any money doing it. Maybe you gave up a large salary to stay home with your children. Perhaps nobody says "thank you" even though you have been serving all day. There can be times when we feel overlooked and upset that there seems to be little reward for all of the time and effort we give.

Yet these verses help us to keep it all in perspective. When you work as unto the Lord, not to men, your reward may not be in physical possessions or money. Your reward, though, will come, and it is the best kind of reward. It is a reward, not of temporary significance, but of eternal significance.

So today, in all that you do, "work at it with all your heart, as working for the Lord." What an amazing privilege to be employed by God himself, taking care of His children.

PRAYER:

God, help me to remember this today—as I serve my family, as I work for their health and well being, I am working for You. You are my boss, the one I report to for duty. You have chosen me for this task of raising my children and leading them to You. Help me to honor You in all I do today, both in my actions and in my heart.

REFLECTION QUESTIONS:

- What advice do you wish someone would have given you before you became a mother?

- Are there any duties you do as a mother that you dread and find yourself having a bad attitude about?

- What types of rewards do you see for your hard work?

_____

_____

_____

_____

_____

_____

_____

_____

_____

_____

_____

_____

_____

DAY 17

Read: Ephesians 6: 10-18

Many children love playing dress up. My friends who have little girls have trunks full of dresses, tiaras, plastic high heel shoes, and lots and lots of glitter. As a mom of two boys, my house has never seen a dress up trunk like that. Our closets are full of ninja costumes, battle gear, cowboy hats, and superhero costumes. My boys have an old Roman soldier costume that consists of a helmet and chest plate, arm cuffs, and a plastic sword. Seeing them wear that costume always reminds me of this Scripture passage.

In Sunday school as children we're often taught about the armor of God, but as adults we sometimes forget about it. We forget that our struggle is *not* against flesh and blood, and that we are in a spiritual battle. There are times when we have bad days and life happens, yet there are also times when the enemy attacks us and wants to distract us from our relationship with God. He tries many tactics to turn us away from God, yet one of the biggest tactics he uses is our own minds.

When we are home with our kids, our minds can easily turn to fear and anxiety over things that might happen, over finances or over decisions that need to be made. If we are not careful, these feelings can cloud our judgment and take our eyes off of our Peace.

Because we are raising children and training them to be like Christ, we can expect opposition from the enemy. It is so important we remember to put on the armor of God daily. When we put the belt of truth on, we can combat the lies of the enemy. When we wear the breastplate of righteousness, our heart will be protected. When our feet are armed with the gospel of peace, God can transform our fears and anxiety. When we take up the shield of faith, we are able to look ahead at what God will do and believe that He will give us the strength that we need. The helmet of salvation and the sword of the Spirit cannot be forgotten either—the very Word of God. When we replace the lies of the enemy with the Word of God, we are able to combat the evil one.

We don't have to remain victims and feel helpless to the attacks of the enemy. God has given us everything we need to stand firm and to fight. Today, remember to put on the armor of God, so you can be spiritually and emotionally prepared to handle whatever comes your way.

PRAYER:

Holy Spirit, arm me with the power I need to stand against the enemy. Remind me to put on this armor every day so that I can combat the lies and the opposition that I will face. Help me to be brave, to rise up against the enemy, and know that I will succeed because You have armed with me with everything I need to stand.

REFLECTION QUESTIONS:

- Which piece of armor listed in the armor of God do you find yourself needing to put on the most?

- Has there ever been a time when you felt attacked by the enemy?

- How might putting the armor of God on each morning change your attitude about the day ahead?

_____

_____

_____

_____

_____

_____

_____

_____

_____

_____

_____

_____

_____

_____

DAY 18

Read: Matthew 7:7-12

Amy's daughter Rachel desperately wanted a new doll for Christmas, one that all her friends had, but Amy and her husband didn't like this particular doll. The doll and the cartoons that accompanied it portrayed attitudes and behaviors they didn't want their young daughter to emulate. After Amy and her husband talked about it, they decided to buy a different gift instead, and tried to explain it to Rachel. Rachel was not happy about it. She whined and complained and even threw in the line "you don't love me!" After a few weeks, Rachel was over it and forgot all about it.

It is frustrating when our kids don't understand the choices we make. They cannot see our perspective; they cannot see the big picture, so they get angry. They don't understand that we love them and are trying to protect them.

Sometimes our relationship with God can closely mirror our relationships with our children. We ask God for things and then get upset when we don't get what we want. We pout and complain and even accuse God of not loving us. We may not understand the consequences of our choices, or the ramifications that may come along with what we are asking for.

This passage reminds us God wants to give good gifts to His

children. Verse 11 says He will "give good gifts to those who ask Him!" So then why doesn't He give us the good things we want, even after we ask Him so many times? Some of those things we ask for really *are* good things, and maybe they are not even for ourselves. Perhaps we've been asking God for a healing, or to provide something that is desperately needed, or for a particular door to open or close.

While we don't understand God's ways or His answers sometimes, we read in His Word that He gives good gifts to His children. We may not understand His answer, but it doesn't mean He has not answered. In verses 7-8, where Jesus is instructing us to ask, seek, and knock, He is not saying that when we open the door, our answer will always be behind it. He is promising that He will always be behind the door. When we knock on that door, He will be there.

No matter what His answer is, even if we don't like it, He will be there, lovingly guiding us through. His good gifts may not be what we expect or even want, but they are still good.

PRAYER:

God, I don't always understand Your ways. There are answers I have been seeking, and I get frustrated waiting for the answers. Help me to be patient and remember You have my best interests in mind. Help me to trust You, even when I don't get the answer I wanted. Thank you for loving me and for all of the good gifts You have already given to me.

REFLECTION QUESTIONS:

- What is something you asked God for that you did not receive?

- What was your attitude when you realized your prayer wouldn't be answered as you had hoped?

- Write down some of the good gifts God has given to you over the years.

_____

_____

_____

_____

_____

_____

_____

_____

_____

_____

_____

_____

_____

_____

_____

_____

DAY 19

Read: Luke 10:38-42

If you have more than one child, isn't it amazing how they can live in the same household and be raised by the same parents, yet have such different personalities? My two boys are complete opposites: One is introverted, the other is the class-clown. One won't touch vegetables, while the other one could happily eat them at every meal. One is a morning person, the other is a night-owl.

Mary and Martha were sisters, yet they seemed like opposites. Martha was the Type-A, woman in charge, hospitable host, working hard to prepare a meal for her visitors. Mary was the Type-B, laid back, "I can do it later" type who just wanted to sit with her guests for awhile. Was one of them right and the other one wrong?

Not necessarily; they were both behaving in the way they were created to be. Yet Jesus looked directly into their hearts—Mary's heart was at rest, while Martha's heart was distracted and frustrated with her sister. It is easy to look at this passage and assume we should all be like Mary and sit at Jesus' feet all the time, but how would we get anything done?

Jesus points out that Mary had chosen what was better (v. 42). Was it better to let her sister do all of the work? No, it was better to let her heart be at rest, and know when to work and when to sit and be still.

As moms, we often struggle with this balance ourselves. How do we get everything done yet still find the time to sit at Jesus' feet? We try to spend time with the Lord, but we get interrupted so often that we just give up. Jesus pointed out that there was a time to work and a time to be still.

Are you making the time to be still? Are you creating time to sit before Jesus' feet, even when there is a lot to be done? This passage doesn't imply you have to sit there for hours and neglect your responsibilities. Mary undoubtedly knew there was much to be done, but her first priority was not those things—her first priority was to listen to Jesus' voice. The rest could wait.

If you are reading this right now, you are making an effort to connect your heart with the Lord's. Yet don't forget to also take a few moments to sit before Him without an agenda, without filing the time with reading and prayer, so you can just stop listen to His voice.

PRAYER:

Jesus, in these moments that I try to carve out of my day to sit at Your feet, help me to remain focused on You. Help me to have an undistracted heart, a heart that is willing to stop everything just to listen, when You call me to do that. I want to create more time to sit at Your feet. Please show me windows of opportunity when I can connect with You, and help me to hear Your voice.

REFLECTION QUESTIONS:

- If you have more than one child, how are they different from each other? If you have one child, how is your child different from you?

- How can you manage getting everything done with sitting still at Jesus' feet each day?

- How do you feel after spending time with God?

_____

_____

_____

_____

_____

_____

_____

_____

_____

_____

_____

_____

_____

_____

_____

DAY 20

Read: Ecclesiastes 3:1-13

When you first become a mother, you realize very quickly there are many people who will give you unsolicited advice. Advice about sleeping, feeding, discipline, you name it— somebody has an opinion. One of the most common pieces of advice I received was "Cherish every moment, because the years fly by." When people said that to me over and over again, I got a little annoyed. I felt like they were not seeing the struggle I was in, and I didn't want to hear about how I needed to plaster a smile on my face and pretend everything was perfect.

Now that my boys are older, the days of potty training, the Curious George re-runs, the walks around the block, the daily nap time struggles, the bath time routines, the tiny socks in the washer, the multiple changes of clothes have passed. We have new routines and new issues to deal with. But now I get it. They are growing very, very fast.

This new stage we're in has great benefits too. They are coming into their own, and it is a joy to watch them grow. There are still tinges of the babies they used to be, like when I was two minutes late picking up my six-year-old from school and he ran to me with tears in his eyes. He still wanted his mama, and it touched my heart. Those little boys are still in there, but I'm learning they desperately want to be big boys, and fast.

One thing I didn't realize until I had been a mom for some time was that motherhood is really a series of seasons. We have seasons of time at home, seasons of busyness, seasons of school activity, and seasons of rest. In whatever season we are in, we can feel like it is taking forever. Yet when we look back, we see how fast it really went.

The writer of Ecclesiastes knew this well. He explains that there are so many different seasons we will face in our lives, but God makes "everything beautiful in its time" (v. 11). In verse 13, though, the writer reminds us that it is a gift from God if we are able to find satisfaction in whatever we do, in whatever season we may find ourselves in.

Whatever season you are in today, ask yourself if you are being content in this season and able to find joy, or if you are just waiting for it to be over. Some seasons are tough to go through, but hang in there, because another one is just around the corner.

PRAYER:

God, help me to find joy in this season that I'm in. I know it won't last forever, although sometimes it feels like it. Thank You for the beauty that You bring in each season I go through. You are right there with me. Help me to find the joy that is waiting for me in this season I am in.

REFLECTION QUESTIONS:

- How would you describe this current season of motherhood you are in?

- What are the particular blessings and challenges of this season?

- What is one way you think you have grown throughout your seasons of motherhood?

_____

_____

_____

_____

_____

_____

_____

_____

_____

_____

_____

_____

_____

_____

_____

_____

Day 21

Read: Colossians 1: 15-23

Do you ever have one of those weeks when everything around you seems to break or fall apart? We had a couple of weeks like that recently. Both of our cars broke down and needed costly repairs. Our backyard grass got a disease in it that spread, so we had to kill all the grass and replant. On our wedding anniversary, our refrigerator broke and we had to live out of ice chests for a week. On top of all of that, our boys' bedroom window broke. All of the repairs were costly and we did not have the money. Have you ever been there?

And yet I also realize that these inconveniences are so minor, they are *first-world problems*, and they are all luxuries. Yet it is still easy to feel overwhelmed by the amount of things gone wrong in the same period of time.

This passage in Colossians reminds us to keep all of this in perspective. Verses 15-17 state that *Christ* is in charge here. By Him *all things* were created—yes, even my car, my refrigerator, my grass, my life. It was through His power these things were made.

"All things were created by Him and *for Him.*" Did you catch that? All these things were not only created by Him, but they were created *for Him*! They were created to give Him glory! How can a material possession bring God glory? Well, it's all about your attitude toward that possession.

How can I bring God glory through the things He has given me? What is my attitude toward these things? Do they own me? Have I made them into gods? Have I let these things replace the joy of the Lord within me? If so, He is not getting the glory.

Our prayers can change from, "God, please fix these things. Please give us the money to deal with all of these messes," to instead, "God, how can we bring You glory through these trials? How can we shift the focus from our possessions back to YOU?"

When little inconveniences have got you down, or when big trials overwhelm you, remember *in Him all things hold together*. We can take the pressure off of ourselves to try to hold everything together; He has already got that covered. The things that are falling apart around us—our bodies, our marriages, our health, our relationships, our finances—*in Him all things hold together*. He sees the big picture, and we can breathe easily knowing He has our lives in His hands.

PRAYER:

Lord, You are in control. I thank You for that, because sometimes everything else seems to fall apart. May You receive the glory through my life and through everything that I own. Help my frustrations not to overrule a thankful heart. All that I have belongs to You.

REFLECTION QUESTIONS:

- What are some inconveniences you are currently dealing with?

- How can your prayers change in regard to those inconveniences?

- What might God be trying to teach you when things like this happen?

_____

_____

_____

_____

_____

_____

_____

_____

_____

_____

_____

_____

_____

DAY 22

Read: John 17:6-19

As mothers, we do everything we can to protect our children from harm. Sometimes we even make decisions based on our own fears that can hold back our children. I remember when my husband and I needed to make a decision about schooling options for our boys. We distinctly felt God was leading us in a particular direction, but it felt very scary—exactly the opposite—of what we wanted to do to keep them safe. I shed many tears over that decision and wrestled with God. I questioned if my husband and I were really hearing God, yet God gently led us through that uncertain door.

As I read this passage, it reminded me of that experience. The passage begins with Jesus praying for Himself, then His disciples, and then for all believers. In the middle of the prayer for His disciples, He asks, "My prayer is not that You take them out of the world but that You protect them from the evil one" (v. 15).

After reading those words, it became clear to me what my prayer for our boys should be—that God would not take them out of the world, but protect them from the evil one. As I prayed that prayer over and over, I saw God supernaturally protect our boys from harm and evil.

It would be nice if we could put our families inside big bubbles to shelter us from the influences we don't like. Yet as our kids grow up and further away from our physical protection, we can rest in the fact God will protect them from the evil one. Our children may still make decisions we don't agree with, but this prayer can bring us comfort that God is watching out for them.

The second part of this prayer says in verse 17, "Sanctify them by the truth; Your word is truth." To "sanctify" means to "set apart." We can also pray that as our children grow, they would be set apart for God, for His purposes. This may not mean they are set apart physically from the world, but rather spiritually—that in the midst of others who may not believe, our kids would have hearts set apart from the rest. Sanctification is a process that does not happen overnight, but God is continually doing His work in our kids' hearts.

Throughout the day today, whisper this prayer to the Lord: that He would protect our children from the evil one, and sanctify them by His truth.

PRAYER:

Lord, today I pray for my children, that You would protect them from the evil one. Protect them from words they may hear that might hurt their hearts. Protect their minds, their bodies, and their spirits from anything that is not of You. Help me to overcome my own fears and to trust that You will be near them, guarding their hearts. Remind me that as they grow and I let them go, Your presence will be near them. Sanctify my children by Your truth; help them to be set apart, and may others see Your love and light in them. Amen.

REFLECTION QUESTIONS:

- What are three things you want to protect your children from?

- How have your own fears affected your children?

- Are there any fears you have that God might be asking you to give over to Him?

DAY 23

Read: Psalm 136

Listening to children's prayers can be the cutest thing. My boys used to have arguments over who would get to pray at dinner, so we started to switch off and take turns. Their prayers would go something like this:

Micah: "Thank you God for our dinner, and our house, and our cat. Amen."

Jaden: "Thank you God for our dinner, and for our house, and our cat, and our driveway. Amen."

My husband and I looked at each other and smiled. "The driveway?" we both thought. Our older son Micah explained it: "He thanked God for the driveway because we get to ride our scooters up and down it when we play outside." Jaden nodded affirmatively.

It got me thinking—am I thankful for the little things like that? Am I thankful for our driveway? Am I thankful for the everyday conveniences that often go overlooked?

Whenever I would take the boys on walks when they were little, it always took a very long time. They would stop and inspect every bug, every little flower, every rock— everything was a new and exciting experience. So often I was hurrying them back home when they wanted to stop and feel, touch, taste, and smell God's creation. The boys always had an attitude of appreciation and thanksgiving for the smallest of things.

I'm thankful for little eyes see things big eyes don't see, and for little hearts who feel things big hearts overlook.

David was a person who continually modeled an attitude of thanksgiving. Even when he was running for his life, hiding in caves from King Saul, David knew how to have a heart of worship and thankfulness.

In this passage, David continually reminds us to give thanks, including thanks for things we might overlook. He ends each stanza with "His love endures forever." We can give thanks to the Lord for everything He has made, because He made those things out of His love for us. Nothing is too small to give thanks for.

As you go throughout your day today, try to give thanks for the seemingly little things: the water that provides nourishment and cleanliness for your family. The refrigerator that keeps your food fresh. The heater that warms your house. The flower that grows outside in your backyard. God's love for you endures forever, and He created good things for you.

PRAYER:

Jesus, You have blessed me with so much, and it is easy for me to overlook the little things. I thank You for Your gifts to me, both big and small. They are evidence of Your love for me. Today I ask that a heart of gratitude would permeate all that I do.

REFLECTION QUESTIONS:

- What is something, seemingly small, that you can thank God for today?

- Besides words, what you do you think is a way you can express your thanks to God for His blessings?

- Do you truly believe that God's love—*for you*—endures forever?

Day 24

Read: Deuteronomy 11:13-21

Does your family have a list of family rules? Although you may not have formally written them down, many families have a list of principles they abide by. Perhaps the family rules include things like: we will treat each other with respect, we will forgive, we will serve others, etc ... Family rules help everyone to be on the same page, to have a guide for what to work toward, and usually represent what the family desires to be.

In Deuteronomy 11, Moses gives the Israelites some "family rules" to abide by. As the leader of over a million people, Moses was entrusted with the responsibility of leading the people spiritually and giving them guidance from God. He ends his message by reminding them to love the Lord their God and serve Him with all of their heart and soul. This is followed by a blessing and then a warning. God would bless His people, but they would be tempted to turn away.

Although we may not be Israelites, these principles still apply to us as God's people. As we love the Lord and serve Him with our lives, we will be blessed for doing so. That blessing may not always be material, but it will be spiritual. We, too, will be tempted to turn away, lured by the promises of happiness through material things, through ungodly relationships, and more.

Moses instructs the parents to teach these things to their children, talk about them all throughout the day, and write them on their doorframes and gates. Moses desired that these teachings would be passed down from generation to generation. He tells the people to post the words of God on their doorframes, their houses, and their gates to constantly be reminded of God's presence in their lives.

This is where we come in today. Our faith has been passed on to us from somebody else, whether it was a family member, a friend, or a pastor or teacher. How are we passing on that same message and legacy to our children? Are we talking about it with our children throughout the day, or leaving that to the Sunday school teachers on the weekends? Are we taking this responsibility seriously, as the Israelites did?

It is the most important responsibility we will have as parents, to pass this legacy of faith on to our children. Let this be our focus today, asking God how we are doing at impressing the hearts of our children toward the Lord, and how we might be able to improve in this area.

PRAYER:

God, I confess that I am weak in following Your ways all of the time. I want to obey You in my heart, but I give in to temptation so often. Please give me creative ways to pass on Your Word to my children, and help me to lead by example. Show me how I can improve in this area and lead my family closer to You.

REFLECTION QUESTIONS:

- What are one or two family rules that you would like to implement?

- What are some temptations that try to distract you from what God wants for your life?

- How can you pass on your spiritual legacy to your children?

_____

_____

_____

_____

_____

_____

_____

_____

DAY 25

Read: Ephesians 2:4-10

The baby name "Grace" has been one of the top twenty baby names for many years. While many parents may choose the name because of famous movie stars such as Grace Kelly, the name has biblical roots. The Latin meaning of grace is "favor" or "blessing," and in the New Testament it is mentioned 156 times.

In the book of Ephesians, Paul instructs us that grace is a gift, given to us even though we don't deserve it. If we could earn it through our works, then we might be tempted take credit for God's goodness to us, so we are given grace as a free gift. Because of this free grace, we should be motivated to serve God and honor Him—not as a way to pay Him back, but as a way to show our value for this gift He has given us.

Grace might be easy to receive, but it is not always easy to give. It is only as we come to understand God's grace for us, the better that we are, in turn, able to give that same grace to other people:

- To other mothers, who may not raise their children the way we do

- To other family members, who we may not get along with

- To our own children, who may test our patience and disobey

- To co-workers, who make mistakes

- To other church members, who ask inappropriate questions (like "When are you due?" when you're *not*)

In verse 10, Paul tells us "we are God's workmanship, created in Christ Jesus to do good works, which God prepared in advance for us to do."

The good work you are doing today might include: six loads of laundry, dinner in the crockpot, and changing a few dirty diapers. And that is okay, because those are the good works that God calls us to do as mothers. "Good works" doesn't just mean spreading the gospel, baking casseroles for other families, or giving money to the needy. The good works you are doing in your home, today, are exactly the good works Christ has created you to do, and prepared in advance for you.

God created you a masterpiece, His work of art, who He created to do good things. Let His grace flow through you today to extend that grace to others through the work of your hands.

PRAYER:

Lord Jesus, You have freely given me Your grace, yet I have the hardest time extending that grace to others around me. Show me how to extend Your grace to others even when I don't feel like it. Help me to receive Your grace in those areas in my life where I resist accepting it.

REFLECTION QUESTIONS:

- What does "grace" mean to you?

- Who do you have the hardest time showing grace to?

- What areas in your life do you struggle with accepting God's grace?

_____

_____

_____

_____

_____

_____

_____

_____

_____

DAY 26

Read: I Peter 3: 8-15

Brenda's twelve year old son came home from school in a terrible mood and they got into a huge argument. It ended with him slamming the door and yelling, "I hate you!" Brenda was livid. She was also very hurt. After all she had done for him, this was how he treated her? She wanted to lay into him something fierce, to set him straight, to punish him for his disrespect and show him who was really the boss. Yet God spoke to her spirit and asked her to bless him. "Bless him?" she scoffed; yet just as she was about to let a bad reaction slip from her mouth, this verse came into her mind—the verse she had gone over in Bible study the week before: "Do not repay evil with evil or insult with insult, but with blessing, because to this you were called so that you may inherit a blessing" (v. 9).

"But how? How do I bless this child who ignores me, pushes me away, and disrespects me almost every day?" she prayed. "Just bless him," was the gentle reply to her heart.

There is power in blessing our children—especially when they least deserve it. Peter tells us we need to "turn from evil to do good ... seek peace and pursue it" (v. 11).

We don't need to be victims to the moods and volatile emotions of those around us. Even when people don't respond the way we want them to and it hurts our feelings, we can still choose to pursue peace. We can still choose to instill a blessing instead of a curse.

If we desire harmony in our homes (v. 8), if we desire to "love life and see good days," (v. 10), the answer is found right in this passage—and it starts with us. When we choose compassion and humility over pride, when we choose to hold our tongues rather than lash out in anger, when we choose to turn from evil behavior and instead do good, this passage says we will be blessed.

Verse 11 tells us we have to *seek* peace and *pursue* it—we cannot expect it to just happen. We have to run after peace if we want it for our families; we have to make choices that will create peace instead of further conflict. Peace definitely will not happen if we always respond in anger to what our children do to us. As we choose to bless instead of curse those who hurt or offend us, we will begin to reap the benefits of peace in our homes.

PRAYER:

Lord, I don't have the strength in myself to bless instead of curse, to respond instead of react. Help me to stop and hold my tongue when I feel I am unjustly treated. Show me the right way to respond. I pray peace over my home today, and may it start with me.

REFLECTION QUESTIONS:

- What is something your child does that gets a reaction from you every time?

- Do you feel you could bless your child the next time he hurts or offends you?

- How can peace in your home begin with you?

_____

_____

_____

_____

_____

_____

_____

_____

_____

_____

_____

_____

_____

_____

_____

_____

DAY 27

Read: Jeremiah 17: 7-8

One year for my birthday, I received two rose bushes I had been wanting to plant in my backyard. I placed them in the same area where they would receive the same amount of sun, although they were about twelve feet apart from each other. A year later, one is a thriving, beautiful rose plant that blooms dozens of roses each summer. The other barely stands one foot off the ground, is brown and sickly, only bloomed one rose all year, and is dying. What was the difference? They were in the same soil with the same sunlight. The biggest difference is that one was closer to a sprinkler than the other one.

We can get by, we can survive, and we can even sprout a rose on a good day if we try. But if we are not planted near the water, we will not thrive. We will not become all that we were meant to be.

Jeremiah tells us when we trust in the Lord and put our hope in Him, we will be like a tree planted by the water. You see, a tree that is planted by the water sends its roots out to constantly draw from it for growth and strength. That is why in verse 8 we read that the tree "will not fear when heat comes; its leaves are always green. It has no worries in a year of drought and never fails to bear fruit."

There are two key words in this verse that stand out—fear and worry. This type of tree "will not fear when heat comes," and, "has no worries in a year of drought." A year is a long time to go without water. But this tree, because it is planted by the stream, has stored up water in its roots to survive. The verse says it will continue to bear fruit. Why? Because it has depended on the stream every day, not just in the dry seasons.

So how do we continually connect to the Source, the Living Water, so we can survive in every season? We stretch out our roots toward Him. We reach for Him. We do everything we can to connect to Him. We can read His Word and be encouraged, and draw from it as a source of our strength. Instead of worrying, we choose trust.

A healthy tree will provide nourishment and shade to those who take refuge under it. As mothers, it is important that we are drawing our strength from the Lord, so those we take care of will also be strengthened. As we trust in the Lord instead of worry, everyone under our responsibility will benefit.

PRAYER:

Lord, draw me closer to Your stream, to Your source of life. I have been dependent on other things for my strength, but all I need is You. I long to run to You, not just when things are going bad, but in the good seasons as well. Turn my fear and worry into faith and trust, as I turn to You, the Living Water.

REFLECTION QUESTIONS:

- What types of things (or people) do you run to for strength?

- Do you feel you are as connected to God as you should be?

- Are you connected to the Source in every season, or just when you are desperate?

_____

_____

_____

_____

_____

_____

_____

_____

_____

_____

_____

_____

_____

_____

_____

_____

Day 25

Read: James 1: 19-26

I spotted her in aisle five, coming toward me fast with her three children. Yelling and yanking them about, her impatience and anger were overflowing. I stepped out of the way as she brushed past me and quietly said a prayer for the three kids. I watched her that morning, as I placed the items in my cart. My heart was full of judgment. I wanted to grab her by the shoulders and shake her, to open her eyes to the horrible way she was treating them. But then I remembered. I remembered all of the times that I had lost it with my own kids, maybe not in public, but in private. I recalled when my words had wounded their little hearts and my impatience had made them feel like they weren't important to me. I was really no better than she.

It would be impossible to ask a mother to never get angry. The amount of responsibility and pressure we face on a daily basis is tantamount to having multiple full-time jobs all at once. There are days when our anger may rise up and spill out onto those we love the most, and days when we will need to ask for their forgiveness.

James understood human nature. He understood our tendency to be angry. We are not alone in this struggle. In this passage he gives us some sound advice—to be quick to listen, slow to speak and slow to become angry" (v. 19).

Instead, we often get it the other way around; we are quick to become angry, quick to speak, and slow to listen. He goes on to say that this anger we all experience, or rather what we *do* about it, doesn't bring about the righteous life God desires for us.

Motherhood is a constant test of our character. All day long we will be tested and tried, and our character will be shaped and molded either for better or for worse. How we respond to situations we face is often a measure of our spiritual maturity. James makes it clear we need to get a hold of our anger if we desire righteousness. Further down in verse 26, James tells us one of the ways we can control our anger is to keep a tight rein on our tongues.

As your patience is tested today, whether by your children or by people you come in contact with, keep this Scripture passage at the forefront of your mind. Anger is something all of us need to work on, and an area that we can achieve victory in. We don't have to yell, accuse, blame, or hurt others when we are angry. God can change our hearts so we can respond in love.

PRAYER:

Lord, I confess to You that I struggle with anger I have even let it get out of control before. Will You remind me of these words when I am in a tough situation and my anger would normally go out of control? Will You teach me how to handle my anger in a right way, so that I can live the righteous life that You desire? Thank You for Your forgiveness and love.

REFLECTION QUESTIONS:

- What situations do you face on a regular basis that make you really angry?

- How do you tend to handle that anger?

- How can you respond differently next time you face one of these situations?

_____

_____

_____

_____

_____

_____

_____

_____

_____

_____

_____

_____

_____

DAY 29

If you have a son or daughter who has ever gone through the "why?" stage, you know how hard it can be to answer all of his or her questions. My three–year-old used to ask questions about every billboard we passed on the freeway: "Why does she look like that, Mommy?" or, "Why does he look so mad?" He wasn't satisfied until I had given him the entire background story on the model or actor portrayed on the billboard. It definitely made car rides interesting.

As we get older, the "whys" change form—we ask "why" about hardships, trials, and suffering. We want to know why God allows bad things to happen. We want to make sense of what happens to us, to know if there is a cause, and if our suffering could have been prevented if we had taken a different course of action. But many times, the answer is "no." We may never know why God permits us to undergo certain trails, and the outcome might have still been the same if we had acted differently.

Job was no stranger to heartache. He had followed God, he had been blessed, he had seemingly done everything right, and yet it was all stripped away. God never gave Job an answer for his suffering; He just reminded Job he was not forgotten.

Job mourned the loss of his family in this passage. All of his sons and daughters were killed by a wind storm. The Bible says Job grieved deeply. As was customary in that time, he tore his robe and shaved his head. But it was what he did next that was extraordinary: he fell to the ground in worship and praised the Lord.

Job didn't praise God for the tragedy that happened; he praised God for being in control and for being worthy of praise, in the midst of the sorrow. He never blamed God for what happened to his family.

Job teaches us we can love God in trials. We can still honor God through heartache. We can worship the Lord through our worst hours. Our love for God should not be dependent on our circumstances, but simply based on who He is.

If you are going through a particularly difficult season, ask God to turn your "whys" into worship. May we be able to say, as Job did in verse 21, "The Lord gave and the Lord has taken away; may the name of the Lord be praised."

PRAYER:

God, I want to be able to praise You in the bad times as well as the good. Even when I don't understand the "whys," will You help me to trust You? Will You help me to worship You as Job did, even in my most difficult seasons? I'm sorry for the times I have chosen anger with You over worship, and pray that You would change my heart.

REFLECTION QUESTIONS:

- When was a time you questioned God?

- Have you ever been able to worship the Lord through a trial or tragedy?

- Do you feel your love for God is based on your circumstances?

_____

_____

_____

_____

_____

_____

_____

_____

_____

_____

_____

_____

_____

_____

_____

DAY 30

Read: Matthew 4:18-22

When you ask your child to do something for you, or to come when you call, it is very refreshing when he listens and obeys the first time. If you have to ask him multiple times, you can tell he either doesn't really want to obey or he is distracted by other things.

Think back for a moment to the time you came to faith in the Lord, and how you wanted to do whatever He asked of you. When I came to that point in high school, I remember saying, "Lord, I'll do anything for you! Here am I, send me!" (I secretly hoped He wouldn't send me to the jungle somewhere, but I was pretty willing to do anything else).

If you are anything like me, perhaps your prayers changed over the years. Instead of wanting to do anything for God, you started to pray safe prayers instead. Prayers like: "God, I will do anything for you, IF..." (it doesn't mean moving somewhere uncomfortable, my children will be safe, it will be in a good neighborhood, we make enough money to have nice things, we are in a great church, etc ...).

When Jesus called the disciples to follow Him, they didn't ask ANY questions. They didn't respond with, "Um, hey Jesus! Where are we going?!" or, "But what about my job?" or, "How are we going to have food and clothing?" They just immediately trusted Him and went. Matthew 18:20 says, "At once they left their nets and followed Him."

Sometimes we can become too comfortable. We don't want to give up our lives for certain things God might call us to do. Sometimes we become too afraid. We don't know if we can trust Him like we used to. After all, we've been hurt. Our dreams of what we thought He was going to do with our lives did not happen like they were supposed to. And now we feel like we can't really trust Him again.

We can learn a valuable lesson from the disciples response— when Jesus called, they were ready to obey. They didn't analyze or linger or pause to think about it. They obeyed because it was in their hearts to do so, and they trusted Jesus.

Let's get back to how things should be. Let's pray some dangerous prayers this week and be willing to obey, no matter what the cost.

PRAYER:

God, help me with my fears. I want to give myself to You fully, to trust You, but I also desire what is safe, and I desire to protect my family. Help me to have the response of the disciples, that when You called, they answered and did not ask questions. Give me a radical, unwavering faith that will listen to Your voice and obey, even when I don't have it all figured out.

REFLECTION QUESTIONS:

- Has God ever asked you to do something outside of your comfort zone?

- Are you willing to do anything God asks of you? If not, what are you unwilling to do?

- How might God want to change your prayers so that they are more trusting and less fearful?

_____

_____

_____

_____

_____

_____

_____

_____

_____

_____

_____

_____

_____

_____

_____

DAY 31

Read: Hebrews 4: 1-11

A few years ago I had a very long bout with strep throat, and couldn't talk above a whisper for almost two months. Lying in bed with a fever for days, I was quieter than ever before. It was emotionally and physically very hard not being able to communicate regularly with my husband and boys.

When you are alone on your bed, left with only your thoughts, you start thinking about who and what are really important in your life. I saved my voice for only those who I cared the most about—my family and close friends. Those conversations were short but encouraging. My kids heard less yelling and nagging, and more "I love you," and "I miss you." My phone conversations were less idle chatter, and full of more encouraging and sweet words. *Sometimes less is truly more.*

I started to think about how I spend my time: so many days spent running here and there and everywhere, mindlessly filling my time with busyness. As my schedule had to be cleared, I saved my energy for the things that were most important to me—time with people I loved.

There were a few nights when I tried to resume normal activities, but the next day ended up back in bed with another fever. Even when I tried to fill my time with good things, my body rebelled against me, saying, "I told you to REST." I did not have the energy to do things I wanted to do—only those things that were the most important. Once again I learned that *sometimes less is truly more.*

We have to learn how to rest before our bodies make us do it. Rest was so important to God that He even took a day to rest Himself. Because He wanted us to know the importance of it, He wrote it right into the Ten Commandments. Rest begins with an attitude of the heart, a peace that comes with not having to accomplish more, but leaving those things in God's hands. Rest teaches us to depend on God.

How do we learn to rest when there is so much to be accomplished, and so many people who depend on us? Hebrews 4:11 tells us that it takes effort to rest; we have to work at it, we have to create time to rest in the midst of our busy lives. Resting in Christ starts with our hearts, trusting God to complete His work in us. As we rest, we obey God, and we set for our families an example of obedience.

PRAYER:

Lord, I want to rest, but I don't always do a good job at it. When my body is resting, my mind is still hard at work. Will You show me how to make resting in You a regular part of my life again? Will You help me to trust You instead of depending on myself to get everything done? I want to set an example for my family of how to rest in You, and I know it begins with me. Change me, Oh Lord, and teach me how to rest in You.

REFLECTION QUESTIONS:

- When was the last time you rested—not just physically, but spiritually as well?

- Do you make time to rest each week?

- How can a mother find time to rest with all that she has to accomplish each day?

_____

_____

_____

_____

_____

_____

_____

_____

_____

_____

_____

_____

_____

_____

A PERSONAL NOTE:

My hope and prayer is that this devotional refreshed your soul and allowed you to hear God's voice. No moment ever spent with God is time wasted, and He will use whatever time you give Him. Please feel free to contact me with your feedback, your story of how God spoke to you, or just to introduce yourself. I would love to meet you. You can reach me through email at jaimie@jaimiebowman.com. Would you also please take a moment to leave a review at www.amazon.com? It would be so helpful as other mothers seek out a devotional to encourage them in their walk as well. Thank you for taking this journey along with me!

VISIT WWW.JAIMIEBOWMAN.COM FOR ENCOURAGEMENT, HOPE, AND FURTHER HELPFUL RESOURCES.

FOR BOOKING INFORMATION, EMAIL INFO@JAIMIEBOWMAN.COM

FIND JAIMIE ON FACEBOOK AT WWW.FACEBOOK.COM/JMEBOWMAN AND ON TWITTER @JMEBOWMAN